The Upside-Down Sloth

By Fay Robinson

Consultants:

Robert L. Hillerich, Professor Emeritus,
Bowling Green State University, Bowling Green, Ohio
Consultant, Pinellas County Schools, Florida

Lynn Kepler, Educational Consultant

ⴹ CHILDRENS PRESS®

CHICAGO

Design by Beth Herman Design Associates

Library of Congress Cataloging-in-Publication Data

Robinson, Fay.
    The upside-down sloth / by Fay Robinson.
      p. cm. – (Rookie read-about science)
    Summary: Describes how the sloth moves, eats, and even sleeps upside down.
    ISBN 0-516-06018-X
    1. Sloths–Juvenile literature. [1. Sloths.] I. Title. II. Series: Robinson, Fay.
  Rookie read-about science.
QL737.E22R63 1993
599.3'1–dc20
                                    93-18981
                                        CIP
                                         AC

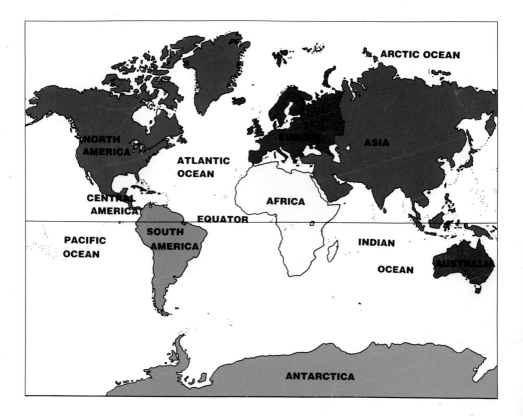

Deep in the jungles of
Central and South America,
the trees are tall and thick.

Shadows cover everything.

Plants grow all around,
making perfect hiding
places for jungle animals.

One of the most unusual
jungle animals is the sloth.

Sloths spend most of their
lives hanging upside down.

They use their hook-like
claws to clamp onto branches.

To travel, sloths move foot
over foot through the
branches – upside down.

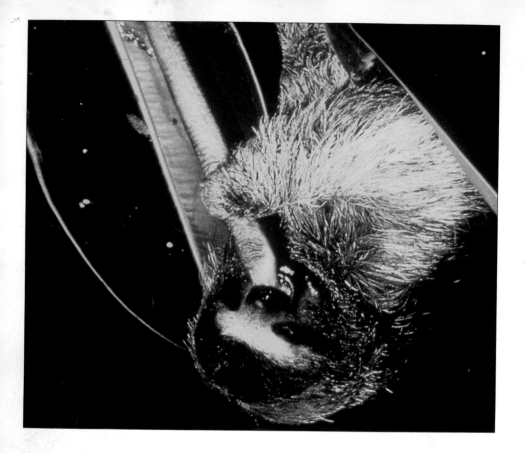

To eat, sloths chomp on
nearby leaves and buds –
upside down.

To sleep, sloths move their legs close together and tuck their heads between them – still upside down.

Sloths spend most of every
day sleeping.

A baby sloth uses its
mother's belly as a cradle.
It clings to her fur with
its claws.

14

When it is nine weeks old, instead of taking its first steps, a baby sloth hangs upside down for the first time.

A full-grown sloth is about two feet long.

18

Sloths move very slowly.
A sloth can take an entire
day to move from one
branch to another.

Try walking across the
room as slowly as you can.
You will probably be
moving faster than a sloth.

Sloths climb down from their treetop homes about once a week.

But they can't walk or even stand up! A sloth's leg muscles are built for hanging, not for standing.

To travel on land, sloths
drag themselves along on
their bellies. This is very
hard work.

But sloths swim very easily.

If you looked for a sloth in
a jungle, you might not
see one.

This is because sloths often look green – the same color as the leaves.

A sloth's natural color is grayish-brown. But millions of little green plants called algae grow in its shaggy fur. This makes sloths hard to see among the green plants.

Animals that might harm
sloths often can't find them.

The sloth is a quiet, gentle animal. The jungle is a perfect place for it to live. In fact, the sloth couldn't live its upside-down life anywhere else.

Words You Know

Map of the World

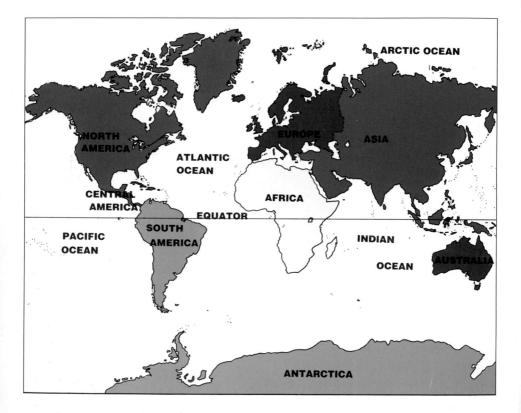

Sloths live in the jungles of Central and South America.

jungle

sloths

claws

algae

cradle

31

Index

algae, 26, 31

baby sloths, 12, 15

branches, 8, 9, 19

Central America, 3, 30

claws, 8, 12, 31

color of sloths, 25, 26

cradle, 12, 31

eating, 10

fur, 12, 26

heads, 11

hiding places, 5

jungles, 3, 5, 6, 24, 28, 31

leaves, 10, 25

leg muscles, 21

legs, 11

map, 3, 30

moving, 9, 19

size of sloths, 16

sleeping, 11, 12

South America, 3, 30

swimming, 23

traveling on land, 22

trees, 3

world map, 30

About the Author

Fay Robinson is an early childhood specialist who lives and works in the Chicago area. She received a bachelor's degree in Child Study from Tufts University and a master's degree in Education from Northwestern University. She has taught preschool and elementary children and is the author of several picture books.

Photo Credits

Animals Animals – ©Michael Fogden, 14, 17, 22, 23; ©Jim Tuten, 20

©Frederick D. Atwood – 7, 11, 31 (center left)

South American Pictures – ©Tony Morrison, 5

Tom Stack & Associates – ©Roy Toft, Cover, 29

Valan – ©Karl Weidmann, 4, 31 (top); ©John Cancalosi, 27

Visuals Unlimited – ©A. Kerstitch, 10, 18

©Norbert Wu – 6, 8, 9, 13, 24, 31 (center right, bottom left & right)

Al Magnus – map 3, 30

COVER: Two–toed sloth